CRUISING CLOSE TO CRAZY

Laura Shaine Cunningham

BROADWAY PLAY PUBLISHING INC
New York
www.broadwayplaypublishing.com
info@broadwayplaypublishing.com

CRUISING CLOSE TO CRAZY
© Copyright 2002 Laura Shaine Cunningham

Cover image © Uros Kovandzic | Dreamstime.com art ID 11646834

First published in *Plays By Laura Shaine Cunningham* in September 2002
This edition: March 2019
I S B N: 978-0-88145-801-5

Book design: Marie Donovan
Page make-up: Adobe InDesign
Typeface: Palatino

CHARACTERS & SETTING

CAROLEE, *female lead, a country singer, age flexible, spirited, close to the edge but filled with talent and feeling.*

EARL WAYNE, *her bus driver, age flexible, a brusque "good old boy".*

NORBIE, *a drummer and would-be lover to* CAROLEE, *age flexible, whiny, eager to please, a cricket.*

HONEY, *high-octane sexy mega singer, age flexible, pragmatic, a bit too sure of herself.*

CHASE, *male lead, age flexible, the real thing, macho magic, sex god, with a husky voice and a way with women, but down, down, down on himself.*

All the action takes place in the bedroom of CAROLEE's *bus, on a road tour.*

Continuous action, 1 hour and 20 minutes.

NOTE

The play can be performed as a straight play, but it can easily be expanded to include a musical cabaret, following CAROLEE's *last line: Songs can be sung, music played, line dancing.*

In a cabaret format, the audience can call for songs, and the cast can sing them, and the evening can be extended in this free-form format. The cast can encore the songs from the play, or sing popular country songs, on demand. Pre-show music can include Country classics, especially those with "Crazy" in the title. The best of these of course is Crazy *by Willie Nelson, recorded by Patsy Cline.*

(The stage is dark, but alive with sound. Highway noise, recorded music. The blast of an air horn triumphs, signaling the arrival of the Carolee Crockett Country tour bus. In the darkness, we hear the offstage voice of the bus driver, EARL WAYNE.)

EARL WAYNE: *(Hooting in delight)* Woooooeeee! Y'all see that? The guy in the V W! I gave him a little squeeze. He's so scared, he doo-ed himself. He can take that V W back where it come from. We don't need it here. *(New, louder tone, calling to* CAROLEE *in the back of the tour bus)* Hey? How's it going back there? We're only an hour late. We'll be at the auditorium in fifteen minutes, and you know it takes you that long to put on your hair.

(Lights reveal the set. The fourth wall is the rump of the country singer's tour bus. The entire rear end of the bus has been transformed into a customized bedroom-dressing room for CAROLEE. *The decor—vinyl bordello. The walls are puckered leatherette and wired—the entire room oozes music from its plastic pores. The room is almost entirely filled by a king-sized bed. The effect of the set is that of a bed, on bus wheels.* CAROLEE, *herself lies in the center of the bed, but is not immediately visible. She is buried under a chiffon mountain of used costumes. Bordering the giant bed, we see the debris of a dozen one-night stands: a tower of take-out chicken buckets, empty soda cans, and gifts from fans. Among the gifts—a toothpick replica of the Grand Ole Opry, a hand-carved bucking horse lamp, and a plaster bust of* CAROLEE. *Upstage right: the vanity and sink, a cosmetics shelf: five identical Styrofoam heads, wearing identical*

blonde wigs. More blonde hairpieces can be seen lying in clumps, like small dead animals on the floor and on top of the bedding. On the shelf—an electric set of curlers are lit and aglow. Stage left and right: the wide bus window-blinds are drawn shut. Center upstage is the single narrow door that connects the bedrooms to the front section of the bus. Sealed off from the outside, the bedroom appears as a bright-colored capsule, travelling at illegal speed into a charted darkness. Carried in the cradle of this capsule, the unconscious CAROLEE *rides toward her destination. Her recorded voice can be heard.)*

CAROLEE: *(Tape. Deep, plaintive)*
You didn't have to leave me tonight…
I was goin' to leave you tomorrow…
Oh, you didn't have to leave me tonight,
I was goin' to leave you tomorrow

(Bus horn punctuates the recording, which fades to an inaudible level.)

EARL WAYNE: *(Offstage. Bellowing voice)* Carolee! It's time! *(New tone, as he addresses another band member,* NORBIE*)* Norbie… Better go back and see…

(The door to the bedroom opens. NORBIE *enters, directly behind the bed. He is nervous as a cricket, with long hair and a permanently worried look. He wears beads, denims, boots, and a bandana. In rhythm with the bus and his own neurosis, he bobs in place, as he speaks.)*

NORBIE: Carole-ee… It's time. We're almost at the auditorium. You want to look your best. *(He addresses the mound of bedding, clothes, and blonde hairpieces.)*

(Pause: the mound twitches.)

NORBIE: You got a new dress. Don't you want to put it on? *(Roots through heap of costumes)* I thought you was saving it special for tonight. *(He smoothes down the wrinkles.)* C'mon, Carolee… You know you only going to get mad at me, you don't get up. *(Whisper)* You know who all's going to be there. This is the big one, Carolee. There going to be ten thousand people there… the T V and everything…. *(Sweeter voice, cajoling)* And you know you ain't going to let them down. Carolee don't do her people that way.

(The mound remains immobile.)

NORBIE: Shit. *(Higher whine)* It just gets harder, the longer you wait. It's just going to make everybody late. *(Pause)* The boys is all ready. It's just you. I know how you feel. You been had.

(The mound [CAROLEE] moves: a spasm.)

NORBIE: *(Softest tone, conspiratorial)* Look, you think I'm looking forward to seeing him again? I'm not crazy. But we can get through it. Then you can go back to bed. *(Sweetest whine)* You been pushing yourself too hard this trip, and there's them don't make it any easier. But you're bigger than they are, you are, you are. And you're almost there. This one time and it's over. *(Luring)* Then you can go to Hawaii—forget all the shit.

EARL WAYNE: *(Booming over sound system)* Just shake her.

(NORBIE tentatively reaches under the bedding, lightly shakes CAROLEE. There is no response.)

NORBIE: *(Whining into intercom)* I can't do nothing with her tonight. You try.

(Sound effect of bus braking, restarting, as another band member takes over the wheel. EARL WAYNE materializes in the doorway. Too large for the dimensions of the room, he appears wedged in the doorframe, and seems to squeeze himself into the space. A heaving fat man, he maintains a Cupid prettiness to his face with kissy Elvis lips and a high pompadour. He wears a cowboy suit, a size too small, and

a steerhorn belt. He stoops slightly under the low ceiling, his pompadour flattening against the tufted vinyl. He bobs alongside NORBIE, *both men bobbing in time with the bus motion.* EARL WAYNE *studies the mound.)*

EARL WAYNE: Well, hell. She couldn't do this when it was just the show, she has to wait for the fuckin' cavalcade a stars, pull this shit on us. *(Yelling)* This ain't just the show, Carolee, this is the fuckin' salute!

*(*EARL WAYNE *scoops up* CAROLEE'*s inert form, raises her, then drops her— dead-weight—to the mattress, then repeats the process, his manner habitual.)*

EARL WAYNE: She's all right. They call her name, she'll come running. *(He eyes the violet dress in* NORBIE'*s hands.)* In her violet dress, with her hair all done. She'll come running when they call her name…. *(He bellows.)* Caroleeee! Ten minutes.

*(*CAROLEE *bolts into a sit-up position on the bed. The covering of the bedding and costumes slide away, to reveal her for the first time. She is a malnourished beauty, her face cadaverous, recalling American Indian ancestry—high cheekbones, slant-eyes, but her coloring Scots-Irish, fair and freckled. Her real hair is as long and blonde as her wigs, but lank, falling to her waist in matted strands. Chalk-white, wearing a wrinkled white nightdress, she looks like a ghost of herself. As she bolts upright, her face appears aligned with the Styrofoam heads: the actual head joining a row of imitations. Her eyes open wide, unseeing, then she slumps backward on her bed.)*

NORBIE: *(Concerned)* I don't know. She looks like she did in Albuquerque.

EARL WAYNE: *(Checking her pulse, routinely)* Ain't that bad. She'll be all right. *(He eyes her hair curler set.)* She turned her curlers on. Just give her five.

(EARL WAYNE *squeezes himself out the door.* NORBIE *hesitates before following.*)

NORBIE: *(Considerate whisper to* CAROLEE*)* Let me know, you need me, hear? *(Soft)* Take five.

(NORBIE *exits. The bus bedroom appears still for one moment, then* CAROLEE *pops up. She furtively surveys the room, ascertaining she's alone. She sits up in the huge bed, confiding—to herself and to the spirits in the room. Her speech has a low rhythm—and almost everything she says, she's said before—her verbal stream of consciousness is a refrain)*

CAROLEE: *(Speaking non-stop, with broken energy)* My mouth's so dry, I can't talk. *(Accelerating)* Nine times in the hospital this year. Nodes. Ain't suppose to sing, that's how come I'm on the road, doing two shows a night, in thirty-six cities. I got letters from doctors all over the world, say, "Carolee, don't sing, don't speak, don't even open your mouth." There 's one doctor so big, he's too big for the Mayo Clinic, that's how big he is, took one look down my throat, and said, "Don't even open your mouth for a year, Carolee, don't speak, even to me." *(Pause)* So I kind of nodded at him, then went right back on the road, I can't do my people that way. God respects you when you work, but He loves you when you sing. *(She roots through the piled bedding.)* Where's my nerve pills? *(She finds a baggie, pops a pill.)* I thank God, I'm not on dope. *(She swallows a few more pills.)* This just Percodan, for my back. *(She takes another one.)* Clears your head real good, too. I just had a sharp thought. *(She blinks.)* It was passing through. *(She shakes her head, woozy.)* Well, it'll come back. Always do. *(She gropes along the vanity shelf, accidentally knocks off one Styrofoam head.)* Didn't like that one much, anyway—I had another kind of nerve pill, it was better than most. It was the only one could stop my bad dreaming. *(She squints at audience.)* You ever dream you were dead?

And it was so real, you was surprised to find you wasn't? Only you wake up, it ain't that different? *(She shivers.)* I have been having dreams so bad, I can't sleep. I'm afraid to put down my head, that's the truth. *(Shudder)* I was wearing my violet dress, I was in a wine-color coffin, in a wine-color room. Everybody in the business come pay their respects. They was all around me, whispering, "Oh ain't it sad, don't she look sweet?" But they was drinking beer and eating chicken legs, too. Earl Wayne. Norbie. The Duker... Honey Bascomb. They was all there, saying how great I was, but it was a bunch a bull. They were all just thinking—"Now, she's dead, even her old albums will sell." *(Thoughtful)* Well, it worked for Elvis. He gone gold. *(Sigh)*

CAROLEE: I had to lie there, listening to all their bull, like they wasn't the ones put me right where I was. And they were saying *(Imitation simper)* "Oh, don't she look beautiful, ain't she finally at peace." Meanwhile, they got the new album piled up outside the funeral home door. Too bad I can't get out of my coffin and sign them. And you know, the entire time, the entire time, I'm just laying there, waiting for him to come in. *(She squints at the audience.)* And you know which one. There's only one ever really makes you crazy. Oh, there's some can get you going, make you a little nuts, but there's only one, can kill you. And don't you know? He don't even show. He done me dead like he done me alive. *(Angry)* And now they want me standing next to him in the auditorium lined up with all a them, so we can be the Cavalcade of Fools.... I can just see it. Him and me, crowned fools of country music, salutin' to our own stupidity. Winding up with Amazin' Grace. *(Croaking lyrics)* " Oh, I'll fly away...." *(Bitter)* I'll fly away, all right. I've flown. *(She shudders.)*

I'm dying. This old bus is going to be my hearse. I'm dying, and there's nobody to care.

(Bus pulls into auditorium parking lot. A loud squeal. Bedroom door opens: NORBIE *re-enters, more anxious than before.* CAROLEE *slumps backward, feigning unconsciousness.)*

NORBIE: We're here—the buses is in. I talked to Barney. It's a full house. Sold out. Everybody's going to get something to eat real quick before the show starts…. They're already off their buses…. *(He peeks out the window blinds.)* Simpson Brothers, Junior Ashcroft, Mississippi Moonshine, Alabama, and that new group, Groundhog…Merle Haggard.

*(*CAROLEE *tenses, waiting for another name.)*

NORBIE: …Honey Bascomb. They're all runnin' in to the steak place next to the auditorium. They have Mex. Let me run, go get you some, get it down fast, so you won't faint like you did in Omaha….

CAROLEE: No… *(She strains, listening.)*

(Sound effect of bus squealing past, a brief musical motif: CHASE's *theme)*

CAROLEE: That's another bus…. Is it…?

NORBIE: It's him.

CAROLEE: Shut them blinds! *(She bolts upright.)*

NORBIE: What's he doin pulling over to us, now? He had his spot.

*(*CAROLEE *is wild, wired, that* CHASE *is now near her.)*

NORBIE: I'll go out and tell him to git. That's one face you don't have to see before the show. I bet he even try to talk to you backstage, you'll spit in his eye and cuss him out good. Nobody'd blame you, you hit him on the head and left him for dead…I'll tell him for you: He can see you on stage, but that's it.

CAROLEE: *(Frantic to stop him)* No! I've never been...a hater. I won't go on with him, but I...might accept...a...formal apology.

(NORBIE moves toward CAROLEE, closing in, suddenly desperate, whining.)

NORBIE: Marry me.

CAROLEE: I told you—I don't believe in marriage.

NORBIE: We could drive to Reno right after the show and be married in a minute. Oh, let's go. Let's just do it.

CAROLEE: Oh, Norbie. Don't start on this... You know my divorce ain't final.

NORBIE: When will it be?

CAROLEE: When I'm dead.

NORBIE: You never see the Duker. It's been years.

CAROLEE: And I'm the one's counting them. I bought him his own town: He can stay in it.

(CAROLEE leans, almost a phototropism toward her shut window blind, in the direction of CHASE's bus.)

CAROLEE: *(Under her breath, to the audience re: CHASE)* He had to come so close to me....

NORBIE: Right after the show, we go to Reno. I bet they can finalize your divorce at the same time: They have chapels for it. *(Kneeling, like a proposal)* Oh, my Darlin, my Baby. Just do the show for me. You know how I love to hear you sing. *(Even more urgent)* Marry me.

(CAROLEE lies back on the bed.)

CAROLEE: You don't want to marry no woman on her deathbed.

NORBIE: It wouldn't be a deathbed, I get in it with you. *(He tries to crawl on to bed.)*

CAROLEE: *(Bristling a bit)* None of the Boys can set in my bed, you know that. And I ain't never singing again. I've sung my song.

EARL WAYNE: *(Off)* Caroleee… We're running out of time! …Is she up?

NORBIE: *(Yelling into intercom)* She's up.

EARL WAYNE: *(Off)* We got company. Some asshole's parked a foot from us: I guess we can just give it a shove when we go….

*(*CAROLEE *rolls over on the bed, to sneak a peek from her lowered blinds: she wants to see* CHASE'*s bus.)*

CAROLEE: You tell him: Get his bus and his butt out of here. *(False fuming)* This lot's only a mile wide, he has to park right next to me. He thinks I'm going to stand next to him and salute him…. This old world's not big enough for him and me.

NORBIE: They're salutin' him and you, Carolee. *(To persuade her)*

CAROLEE: …for our goddamned duet.

NORBIE: Mostly they come to hear you. It's you made it such a hit— "You're no better than you ought to be… but you're good enough for me!"

CAROLEE: Where my nerve pills?

NORBIE: You're holding them. *(Persuading her, harder)* Everybody's come to see you. They're not interested in him. It's you. Those are your fans out there.

EARL WAYNE: *(Off. Bellowing)* Carolee? Norbie? What's goin' on back there?

CAROLEE: Tell him. Tell him I ain't goin' on.

NORBIE: *(Fake, into intercom)* She's looking much better. She's getting ready. *(Whisper to* CAROLEE*)* I know you won't let everyone down….

CAROLEE: *(Muttering to herself)* I could just take a bottle and break it over my head.

NORBIE: *(Louder, phonier, into intercom)* I'm helping her with her hair!

(Intercepting CAROLEE's grab for a bottle:)

NORBIE: Don't do that! All you need is something to eat! Then you'll be able to get up on your feet! You ain't et since Arizona. And then it was only a little bit a that cold chili, and a tiny bit a popcorn. No wonder, you feel kind of weak. *(Into intercom)* She just needs food! Get her a burrito... *(To CAROLEE)* Beef or cheese?

CAROLEE: I'm done eating.

NORBIE: *(Yelling to EARL WAYNE on the intercom)* Two beef burritos and maybe a Chile relleno if they have it with cheese... *(Most urgent whisper to CAROLEE)* Nothing matters to me but you...I love you. You know I love you.... Can't you feel me, loving you?

(CAROLEE and NORBIE have eye contact as EARL WAYNE's voice bellows back.)

EARL WAYNE: *(Off)* You want refried beans with that?

NORBIE: No, just a Coke. *(To CAROLEE, the romantic whisper)* Just let me touch you, let me touch your hair.... Please, eat something. Them nerve pills won't take on an empty stomach. They work off fat. Just do this much for me...for my lifetime of loving you.

CAROLEE: You know so much. *(Weak)* Well, all right, maybe a piece of coconut cream custard pie.

NORBIE: *(Triumphant yell to intercom)* And one piece of coconut cream custard pie.

CAROLEE: I won't even be able to touch it; you can have most of it.

NORBIE: And while we're waiting for the pie, I'll put these hot curlers in your hair.

CAROLEE: You can throw them curlers out the window—I'm never putting them on again.

NORBIE: Okay. We can do it like we did in Albuquerque: We use the curlers on one of your wigs, and we hide all your own hair.

CAROLEE: You can cut my head off. I'm not going on.

(EARL WAYNE blares through intercom.)

EARL WAYNE: Wooooowwwweeeeeee! Look who's come visiting on our bus!

(CAROLEE, NORBIE stiffen.)

CAROLEE: It's that Chase McCain: tell him to get his butt back where it belongs…. Let him rot in hell.

EARL WAYNE: *(Off)* It's Honey, Carolee…. And she's in her costume: She has to talk to you….

CAROLEE: *(Crushed it's not CHASE. Screaming)* Well tell her, my mouth's so dry, I can't talk! *(She feigns another collapse, burying her face in the covers.)*

EARL WAYNE: *(Off. Nonplussed)* She 's coming back to your room. She can help you get ready. We're going to the restaurant. We'll be back with your coconut cream custard pie.

NORBIE: *(Pleading into intercom)* And two beef burritos, one Chile rellenos if they got cheese and a Coke. *(Referring to CAROLEE)* Two Cokes.

CAROLEE: *(Correcting the order, low whisper to NORBIE)* Diet Pepsi!

EARL WAYNE: We'll be back in a couple a minutes. When we do, I want to see you in that dress. *(To NORBIE)* If she ain't in the dress, we got to give her the needle.

CAROLEE: Well, who does she think she is, coming to set on my bus? Who asked her? She don't invite me to her home, and we live in the same town…. *(Imitating a higher, sweeter voice—*Honey's*)* "Me and Max aren't party people. We're real private. We need time just to be human beings." Human beings weren't born with boobs that big. And I'll just bet you she'll just happen to have with her, her new song…. She wrote it while she was crossing the parking lot—I don't have time to listen to it. I don't have time for this shit, I really don't…. She get any more full of herself, her boobs will blow up…

(There is a loud knock.)

Carolee: *(Hiss to* Norbie*)* Tell her to git. Tell her I got nodes. Tell her I'm sick. Tell her I'm dying. Tell her I'm dead already. Tell her I don't want to see her painted up little face in my room…pretending she's twenty when everybody knows she'll never see forty…again.

*(*Honey Bascomb *bursts into the room. She is a many-splendored thing; in full sequined regalia: sparkling costume top over skin-tight white satin pants, with nothing underneath but her ample, cleaving buttocks. She has packaged herself in a glittery wrapper. She is pretty and bright, with the artificial beauty of some tropical bird. She is genuinely animated, but below her surface vivacity, beats a cold, pragmatic heart. She carries a large makeup case.)*

Carolee: *(Recovering her social poise)* Honey! Ain't you sweet? You're looking so pretty. You'll have to excuse me: My mouth's so dry, I can't talk. I got nodes. Nine times in the hospital this year. There's a doctor—he's too big for the Mayo Clinic, that's how big he is—he says, "Don't even open your mouth."

Honey: *(Talking fast: she's in high gear for her show: she's on first.)* I saw that doctor. He don't know shit about singing. Don't you pay him no mind. I have my formula with me…you just sip this… *(She whips out a bottle)* …it's honey and my secret ingredient, sip it straight from the bottle I don't mind your mouth…. You'll never feel the pain. *(She approaches the bed, and pulls forth another jug: Cheramino liquid protein. She teeters on her high heels and seems about to invade the bed.)* You don't mind if I borrow some hair spray…. Wouldn't you know I run out….

(HONEY *finds a can on the bed, then blasts her head, leaving* CAROLEE *and* NORBIE *blinking in the scented, chemical draft. Finished with the spray, she turns, displaying her buttocks in the taut satin pants.).*

HONEY: Well? Would you know me? I ain't been this weight since some cennential.

CAROLEE: You look well.

NORBIE: *(To* HONEY*)* You didn't look so bad before.

HONEY: *(Automatically kissing* NORBIE *hello)* It's good to see you, Norbie; I heard you joined the band. *(Returning to body talk with Carolee)* I lost forty pounds. Ten to go.

NORBIE: *(Trying to get into conversation)* You didn't look so bad before. *(To* HONEY*)* Carolee's running behind. I'm trying to get her dressed.

HONEY: *(More to* CAROLEE*)* Well, I look great naked and standing up—it's when I sit. *(She gestures to the violet costume on the bed.)* You better put on your dress…. It's almost ten to.

NORBIE: And she has to eat something.

HONEY: *(Proffering her jug of Cheramino)* Here. It's all amino acid. Made from bones. It tastes terrible. Try some.

CAROLEE: I'm done eating.

HONEY: I'm so nervous tonight I could wet my panties if I had any on. This is the first time for my new band on such a big show. I been keeping' them hid, till they was broke in. *(New look to* NORBIE*)* What do you think of Sammy on guitar?

NORBIE: *(Distracted, and trying to guess the right answer)* He's not bad. We got to do something with her hair.

HONEY: *(Dead serious about her business)* You can tell me what you really think.

NORBIE: I thought he was good. He sounded good. I'm worried about Carolee. She won't put her hair up, or her makeup on….

HONEY: Better than my Daddy?

NORBIE: Well, different from your Daddy. It's her…. I'm worried about Carolee… You'll be fine.

HONEY: In what way? Different how? In what way different?

NORBIE: Well, more mellow but less laid-back. He's got more underneath. Listen, I have to help Carolee.

HONEY: I hope people won't think now I'm crossing over too much. Well, you tell me tonight. I'm going to rock 'em a little.

NORBIE: Oh, you're always real. I'm sure you'll be real tonight.

HONEY: I want it to be real. That's why I had to do what I did. It was the hardest thing I ever had to do…but they weren't going where I was going. They weren't dreaming, what I was dreaming. We were movin' away from each other in opposite directions. *(Running out of steam)* I didn't want to fire my father.

*(*CAROLEE *perks up a bit, eyes the audience.)*

CAROLEE: *(With whispery fake sweetness)* And your brothers and your sisters?

HONEY: They had their own plans. They'll cut their own records…someday. *(Changing topic, to* CAROLEE*)*

But I got myself in a tizzy for tonight. At least my family was…familiar. I'm taking a chance tonight, with a new band, new songs…. I wrote one this morning…. It was in my head, while I still lay in my bed. I reached for a piece a paper, and wrote it down quick…before it got away. Tell me what you think and if I should do it tonight…if I have to do…an encore.

NORBIE: We don't have time. Carolee has to do up her hair, makeup and put on her dress….

CAROLEE: It don't matter; I ain't goin on.

(HONEY *is shocked, stunned from her self-involvement.*)

HONEY: You don't mean that! This is your tribute! The salute is to you and Chase. The rest of us is out there, paying tribute…. *(Harder)* If you ain't coming out, none of us can salute you!

CAROLEE: Well, I ain't. I had a dream tonight that I was dead. I was wearing a violet dress, and I was lying in a wine-color coffin in a wine-color room…. *(Frightened by the auditorium on her T V monitor)* Is that a wine-color auditorium?

NORBIE: It's blue. *(Frantic, to reassure her)*

CAROLEE: Well I was in a wine-color coffin…. And I was all stiffed up, with a painted-on smile. And when I woke up, nothing was any different; I felt the same. You know what I'm saying?

NORBIE: I hear you, I hear you.

HONEY: Take something for it—take a Midol. Midol and Zoloft go good with a few nerve pills and maybe a cold beer.

CAROLEE: I gone past medicating.

HONEY: Well, we can all do a medley a your songs, and you can just stand there for a minute at the very end….

NORBIE: It could come down to that.

HONEY: That's right! You won't even have to use your voice! Though if you just try that Midol, you'll be surprised at the energy from inside…

(CAROLEE *moans, curls into bed.*)

NORBIE: Try it. Wash it down with a cold beer. Then if you can get some of that coconut cream custard pie in you. You need real food. You'll be able to get up and give the best show you've ever given….

CAROLEE: I got nodes. I been nine times in the hospital this year, and doctors all over the country say "don't even speak." I got a prescription for a brain pill that will put me out for a week. I got it from a doctor who's so big, he's too big for the Mayo clinic, that's how big he is.

HONEY: *(Giving orders to* NORBIE *as she seizes control)* You go get that cream pie: I'll take care of this.

NORBIE: I don't want to leave her….

HONEY: *(Under her breath)* Go before we have the biggest disaster in the history of country music! I don't care if she's unconscious, she's going to get up on that stage! She's got a real weird look to her tonight, but I've worked with worse…. *(More normal tone)* Get out of here, Norbie. This is a woman's thing to deal with. We're going to talk dirty, you don't want to hear it. You come back with that cream pie, she'll be all dressed and ready to go…. You go on. Leave to me. I am famous for never failing.

NORBIE: *(Bowing out)* You're fine people.

(NORBIE *exits, leaving* HONEY *to minister to* CAROLEE. HONEY *offers her the throat syrup.*)

CAROLEE: My mouth's so dry, I can't talk. I'm dying tonight. I seen it happen already…I was lying in a wine color coffin…in a wine-color room…. *(She breaks off into a new idea.)* Do you believe in precognition?

HONEY: I ought to. I knowed when I was in trouble. And I know you got to get up off this bed and out of the bus!

CAROLEE: Things happen in your head before they happen to you for real?

HONEY: All the time. This song I'm going to try out tonight…. I heard it before. Maybe in another life. *(She hums a tune: a wistful ballad.)*

CAROLEE: *(Picking up the melody)* "It would still be you…. If I knew a thousand men, in the end, it would still be you…. If I lived and loved and married again, in the end…it would still be you…" *(New tone, more dazed than irritated)* Hey, that's my song.

HONEY: "It Would Still Be You" …is yours?

CAROLEE: That was my last single!

HONEY: Then how'd it get inside my head?

CAROLEE: *(Oddly not angered but warmed by the plagiarism)* Well, maybe it was subconscious. You n' me…we're like sisters. We look and sound just alike. *(They don't. To audience)* Now she's here, she ain't so bad.

(HONEY unfurls a paper towel, reads her handwritten lyric.)

HONEY: "If you were worse than you are…. If you walked harder across my heart…. If we were always apart. It would still be you…."

CAROLEE: That's a little different but in a way it's the same. *(She pats HONEY.)* It's all right: I got the copyright. Now just don't tell me *I Call My Pain by Your Name* is yours, too.

HONEY: No, it's yours. The *Hurt Me* album. We both made out on that one. You should have stuck with me. We harmonize so well. Everybody's always begging us to cut another album together. And tonight, you know they want to see us together again. Come do it for me, Carolee…. So it can be like it was when we were on our own tour….

CAROLEE: You can sing without me, Honey.

HONEY: Not tonight, I can't…. Come on; we'll do my new song as a duet…. Maybe I'll even give you half credit. You sounded pretty good, just now, I think your voice is fine.

CAROLEE: Save your breath, Honey. I'm not going with you, or anybody to sing….

HONEY: *(Pouting)* Even though you know I need you tonight. With a new song, and a new band—you got to help me out. Without you, there's no show, you know that! The whole country's set to honor you n' Chase; it's gonna be taped, for Crissake! You got to come out so we all can sing to you!

(HONEY sees CAROLEE flinch at the name "Chase".)

HONEY: It were him, weren't it? You should never have mixed it up with that Chase McCain…. It were him, weren't it?

(CAROLEE drinks the cough syrup.)

CAROLEE: Don't hurt, don't hurt a bit.

HONEY: I told you not to work with him. *(She uses a new tone, as she resumes a favorite theme.)* Men. Crazy old men. All they know is they got a long thing and you got a hole to put it in. Crazy old men. Some nights, don't you just want to bite it off?

CAROLEE: I'm not a hater.

HONEY: But you can't let a man ruin your life, spoil a whole show…that, in the end, could give pleasure to millions of people all over the world.

CAROLEE: You don't need me. You'll do fine. *(Changing the subject)* How's Max?

HONEY: He's home. He's fine. We can catch up after the show. Right now, just let me put these curlers in your hair.

(CAROLEE *pushes away the curlers.*)

CAROLEE: I ain't seen the Duker in a year. He's raising beef cattle. He ships 'em. I don't want him killing on my farm. I don't do my cattle that way. Even if I ain't there to see it: They go. What's Max doing?

HONEY: (*Impatient, trying to fluff* CAROLEE's *hair*) He's in business for himself: Septic.

CAROLEE: That's good.

HONEY: Come on, now, you'll feel better if you just put on some lipstick and blush-on.

CAROLEE: You're really happy with Max?

HONEY: We love each other; after ten years we can just love and pet for two hours before we get started. That's how I like it. If a man ain't tender, I kick him in the balls.

CAROLEE: Does it work?

HONEY: Well if it don't, I don't have to worry about it, do I? You don't see me, lying and crying in my bus, do you? You going to let Chase McCain do you like this? Don't you think should get up there, just to show him...*show everybody*...You don't care! You're bigger and better than he ever was!

CAROLEE: I can't. I can't get up there with him! It was ...too much with him... You don't know what he's like... You ain't been with him (*Caught short by a new doubt*) ...Have you?

HONEY: I don't know if I have or I haven't. I forget. (*Smile*) There been a few.

CAROLEE: If you forgot him, you never knew him.

HONEY: Well, you don't have to eat an apple to know it's gone bad. I took a look. Sure. He's something. And he knows it. To me, he has a dirty look.

CAROLEE: *(An involuntary defense)* He's clean! He takes a lot of showers, and his hair's always washed.

HONEY: I didn't mean dirty that way. I meant it the other way. He's no dresser, though. I'm sick a seeing him in his tee shirt and jeans. I swear that tee shirt has had the same holes in it for five years…. He had holes in his shirt when he did *Loner*. And he's only worth how many million dollars.

CAROLEE: He's just different, that's all. He's different from the others. They wear studs—he don't wear studs. They wear rhinestones, he don't wear rhinestones. He likes to be just…plain.

HONEY: He could spend three dollars on a new shirt and give us a break. And get himself another pair of jeans.

CAROLEE: Well, I know he's bad, but he looks good in his jeans. They're just so worn and soft….

HONEY: When they're built, they get away with a lot. His kind. That's the worst. Snake hips. That's what he is. That's how Lucifer appears to Woman. Snake Hips. You read your Bible, close, you'll see what they're really talking about… You see a man grow wide as his hips is narrow, run and hide. That man is the Devil and he going to ride you straight to hell….

CAROLEE: I know: You're right. He left me for dead.

HONEY: They say he takes two women a night. One after each show. Not two together. One each time. He likes his privacy.

CAROLEE: He's a very private person.

HONEY: Considering he slept with half the world…
(New squint at CAROLEE*)* It true what they say about
him?

CAROLEE: Whut?

HONEY: They say he goes six times without stopping.
He that way with you?

*(*CAROLEE *refuses to answer.)*

HONEY: Well, you went on tour with him…. You done
fourteen cities. He that way with you?

CAROLEE: *(Shy, but bragging)* I ain't saying.

HONEY: *(Appraising the situation)* It was good; that's
why it's bad.

CAROLEE: *(Breaking down, a bit)* I can't come back from
it, Honey, I just can't…. He took everything from me
when he went.

HONEY: Well, then you just have to get him back. I can
tell you how. I know his kind. He may be the Devil,
but even the Devil can be tamed. You ride him harder
than he rode you: You crack the whip! You don't take
nothing from him! You stay on top. He thinks he can
have you—he come running…. You just got to play it
hard to get….

(As HONEY *speaks, she excitedly works the hot curlers into
a wig and adjusts* CAROLEE *on the bed, so that she can "do"
her hair. Yanking a comb through her hair, then setting the
straggled locks on more hot rollers)*

CAROLEE: Well, how can I be hard to get when I been
got?

HONEY: It's in your head, how he sees you. You don't
give an inch.

CAROLEE: I can't!

HONEY: You got to turn it around. The one thing I won't tolerate is negativity. You think positive—you be anything, you have anything or anyone you want.

CAROLEE: Well, maybe he did like me a little? He wouldn't a done some of what he done, or said some of what he said, if he didn't like me just a bit? Would he? *(Losing herself in reverie)* You ever see a beautiful man go meek—you know—just before—go all shy on you and look down at his feet?

HONEY: *(Working the hair curlers, distracted)* A beautiful man? No. The homely ones go meek all the time. *(With bobby pin in her teeth)* They ought to be meek.

CAROLEE: Well, it was really something. It was so sweet, it hurt me to see it. *(Gaining strength)* Well, he must have liked me then…

HONEY: Of course he did. Now all you got to do is call his bus and tell him: "Get your arse over here, Shithead. I got something to say. And if I don't say it before the show, I'm going to say it during, so a couple thousand people can hear it live and millions more on tape." …He'll be here before these curlers are cool.

CAROLEE: Well I got nothing to lose. I lost it all in Albuquerque.

HONEY: Just don't you dare give him none before the show. You make his old tongue hang out for it. If you give him some, he'll be cracking the old whip again. *(Muttering her theme again)* Crazy ole mens. He'd screw a snake if you held its head down. Pussy's pussy even if it's on a cow. Oh, some nights, don't you just want to bite it off? *(She bites thread off CAROLEE's costume.)* Don't let him even touch you down there. Make him wait. Wait till after the show. *(She fixes CAROLEE's hairdo.)* It's easier on your hair that way too.

CAROLEE: Will you do my face?

HONEY: I know just how. A little lipstick and blusher… there. (*She slaps on the makeup. Surveys her work*) Now you look human. Now watch you don't get this makeup on the dress. (*She prepares to slip the dress onto* CAROLEE.) If you do, you can get it off with Wisk. It's saved me hundreds of thousands of dollars. I used to have to throw them out… If he kisses you, make sure you put on new lipstick, before you go out—don't you dare give him more n' a kiss! Sex is death on makeup. Now get yourself out of this nightgown and put on your dress…

(HONEY *helps* CAROLEE *out of her nightgown and into the dress. As the dress is lowered over* CAROLEE's *exposed, vulnerable body,* HONEY *gives the other woman a critique.*)

HONEY: Your boobs is slipping….

CAROLEE: I know. That doctor in Vegas didn't know what he was doing. In another year, I'll have one boob down to my belly.

HONEY: Well, don't think about it tonight; we can push it up where it belongs…. (*Caught by surprise*) I didn't know you had your kids by Cesarean.

CAROLEE: Only the first two. I was too young, too small. You can hardly have them when you're only twelve, you know. But I had the other two natural. My bones spread apart each time….

HONEY: Don't think about your kids now. They're all growed. You have to concentrate on yourself, tonight.

CAROLEE: I know. I didn't know nothing when I married The Duker. I thought you was supposed to bleed every time.

HONEY: Don't brood on it. Crazy-old mens… All they know is they got a long thing…and you got a hole to put it in.

CAROLEE: Well, I bought him his own town; he can stay in it.

HONEY: You look good now, I don't know why you just don't divorce him.

CAROLEE: I don't know myself. I guess I thought—well, they're all assholes. I know this asshole.

HONEY: He'd screw a snake if you held its head down. Pussy's pussy, even when it's on a cow…

CAROLEE: *(Referring to the grooming)* Take it easy! You're pulling my skin! *(Looking down at herself)* Sometimes I think my skin's grown a size large: it just hanging there like last year's costume. Yeah, a size large.

HONEY: Well, at least you're skinny. I can't eat again until a month from tomorrow…and then not real food. No fried. *(She zips the costume.)* Here. You're done up. Now call Chase McCain and get over with…

CAROLEE: I can't!

HONEY: Well all right, I'll do it. *(She whips out her personal phone, which she wears in holster.)*

HONEY: I got the asshole on my speed dial. *(Into her phone)* Hey…. who's this? This is Honey. Yeah, I'm on Carolee's bus. Who's this? Breadman! How are you, you old fool? Is the man there? Yeah. *(A pause as* CHASE *is presumed to get on)* Hey, Sugar. I'm looking at that mean old black bus a yours. You better get your arse right over here onto Carolee's bus, if you know what's good for you. Great. Love ya. *(She hangs up, turns beaming to* CAROLEE.*)* See, that weren't so hard, was it?

CAROLEE: You're something. I wish I could be like you. Casual… Men love you when you're casual.

HONEY: It's not love it's fascination.

(Her holster phone shrills. Talks into phone)

HONEY: Yeah, I know. I'm on my way. Hold yer water. *(To* CAROLEE*)* Well, there's my call. I got to get backstage. I'm one of the first to honor you. Don't worry, I'll warm them up good…. *(She gives a final fuss to* CAROLEE *and fluffs herself.)* Well, Annie Oakley weren't nothing! There could be a prettier girl singer than you—I don't know who.

CAROLEE: I love you for this, Honey.

*(*CAROLEE *and* HONEY *embrace, careful not to muss one another's hair and makeup.)*

HONEY: Just don't back down. You do as I say, it'll work out. First, just ream him out. Call him twelve kinds of assholes.

(Her phone shrills, shrills.)

HONEY: That'll put him on his best behavior. When he tries to grab you, just put him off. After the show: You can go to bed with him, if you still feel the overpowering urge, but on your terms. You never let him take over! And remember, the whole time: you're in the top ten and his last two albums didn't sell! *(She heads for the door.)* I'll see you for the finale. And I want to see you looking as good as you're feeling!

CAROLEE: *(Excited, leading her to the door)* You will! And I thank you from the bottom of my heart!

HONEY: *(Bowing out)* It was to be expected. I am famous for my kindness. *(She exits.)*

CAROLEE: *(Smiling, nodding)* Don't hurt, don't hurt a bit.

*(*CAROLEE *goes to sit rather primly on her bed. In her violet dress, she looks like a girl waiting for her date. Her expectation makes her younger, more girlish than before. There is a loud knock at her bedroom door.)*

CAROLEE: *(Trilling, breathless)* One second! Well…all right now. Come on in…

(The door opens: admitting the bulk of EARL WAYNE *and* NORBIE, *holding the take-out dinner.)*

CAROLEE: *(To herself)* Shit. *(To* EARL WAYNE *and* NORBIE*)* What are you all barging into my room? You know I'm getting ready for my show. I'm only an hour behind!

*(*EARL WAYNE *and* NORBIE *look at one another in total surprise. They also look relieved, and* EARL WAYNE *sets down a hypodermic needle.)*

EARL WAYNE: *(To* NORBIE*)* I guess we won't need the needle.

NORBIE: *(To* CAROLEE*)* Look at yourself. You look so great. God I can't take my eyes off you!

CAROLEE: Well, I'm not finished dressing and a person could use a little privacy. You come get me when it's time for me to go on. You all should be backstage…. The Boys need to set up….

NORBIE: I got you a lemon pie…they didn't have coconut cream. And a root beer… They didn't have Diet Pepsi.

CAROLEE: Well give me the pie; I'll nibble a bit, and you two go on….

NORBIE: Can I just keep you company a minute? I brought over my burrito and the Chile relleno— they had cheese….

CAROLEE: *(Not wanting him to be there when* CHASE *comes)* We'll do that another time, Norbie…. Right now I need to stay by myself…to prepare.

NORBIE: You expecting somebody?

CAROLEE: I ain't saying.

EARL WAYNE: Well, hurry it up, everybody else's backstage already. We'll be back for you at a quarter to…. That's when they bring you on…. There'll be a medley. The order a songs is the same as we said….

You start off with *You're No Better Than You Ought To Be*...come out on..."But you're good enough for me..." You've only done it a hundred times, you should be all right.

CAROLEE: Fine! *(Leading them out the door)*

(EARL WAYNE leaves. NORBIE lingers.)

NORBIE: I got a queer feeling I shouldn't leave you: You were feeling so poorly before. You been pushing yourself too hard this trip, and there's them don't make it any easier....

(CHASE's theme, three musical chords, sounds. CHASE enters. He is as attractive as one would expect— Very masculine, somewhat scruffy. He has an athletic build and is dressed as predicted: in jeans and a tee shirt. As sexually attractive as he is, his mouth is set and his eyes, glary. He is formidable in his contained anger and noticeably charged up for his oncoming performance [both onstage and here in the bus]. He has been smoking dope, and is, in fact, still smoking it: the joint cupped in his hand. He carries a guitar, in case, and wears old scuffed boots. He stops in the doorframe and NORBIE, seeing him, is rooted to the spot. The two men stare at one another. CHASE delivers his lines like submachine fire: low, deadly without ever having to stop to reload. NORBIE twitches.)

NORBIE: Ole Buddy...

CHASE: *(To CAROLEE, with cold sarcasm)* After everything you done, there's one thing I should thank you for... *(Eyeing NORBIE)* ...and that's for taking my drummer. *(Beat)* We sound a lot better without him.

NORBIE: You do sound better without me! Your last album was great!

CHASE: Columbia dumped it. I guess they were afraid to distribute it, it might sell a few million copies.

NORBIE: Everybody in the business loved it.
Everybody's been saying it's unfair. (*He offers* CHASE *his
hand.*) No matter what went down in Albuquerque…
you know I'm still your buddy, and your music—well
that's hands off. Man, you know I think you're one of
the great people, y'are, y'are!

CHASE: (*Low but final*) I'm going to count to five and
when I hit five, I don't want to see you standing in this
room.

NORBIE: I hear you….

(NORBIE *flees, spooked as a jack-rabbit.* CAROLEE *has frozen
in place on her bed.* CHASE'*s actual presence, his anger
paralyzes her. He moves in for the kill. Underneath his
hostility, there is a sexual charge, long ago explored but not
yet exhausted. He needs to conquer, to control her in every
way.*)

CHASE: (*Quiet, but firing each word as a deadly weapon*) I
heard the latest. That you're trying to kill the salute to
you an' me.

(CAROLEE *makes a low squeak.*)

CHASE: Don't argue with me, Carolee. I didn't come
to continue the fight. I just come to set the record
straight…. (*He shuts his eyes, rocks, as if in contained
pain.*) I didn't think you would do me the way you
done.

(CAROLEE *jerks, a fear reflex.* CHASE *ticks off the list of
grievances.*)

CHASE: One, I didn't think you'd take off with my
drummer. Two, I didn't think you'd badmouth me in a
song. Three, I didn't think you'd run out on me when I
needed you. And Four, I didn't expect you'd sue me!

(CAROLEE *looks flabbergasted.*)

CHASE: And I made up my mind, after that last tour, that there's two things I will never do again, and that's drink while I'm on tour, and sleep with a girl singer. That would never happen to me now…be fooled the way I was…. And it wouldn't have happened to me then, if I hadn't been drinking. But I haven't had a drink in… *(He pauses for emphasis.)* …forty-four days, in order to be ready for tonight and my head is real clear now and I see everything, the way it was…and is. *(He takes a toke from the joint.)* I don't know why I had to go around anesthetized the way I did. I must have been in even more pain than I knew…. *(Eyeing* CAROLEE *in utter hurt)* But you. I didn't think you would do me like you done. I had to cut a single to get rid of the bad feelings…. I was going to sing it tonight.

CAROLEE: *(Open mouth to audience)* I can't believe this…. Can you?

CHASE: I almost died.

*(*CAROLEE *starts: What?)*

CHASE: You can kick a man only so hard, when he's down. If you ask me to forgive you, I know, Lord that I should. I should turn the other cheek but I don't know if I have that kind of strength. I only know…. *(Sweet, meek look)* I'm trying.

CAROLEE: *(To herself, the audience)* I'm trying to remember what Honey said I'm supposed to say….

CHASE: You can't even admit your sin. You can't say: "Forgive me, Lord, forgive me for what I done." I guess there's some past saving. *(He eyes her directly for the first time.)* Cat got your tongue?

CAROLEE: *(Barely audible, a sincere reading of this line for the first time)* My mouth's so dry, I can't talk.

CHASE: And now this. Now, you have to spoil this show, too. Shit, I spent the last year honoring every

asshole in the business…. Next, they want me to honor
Bobby Vinton. Bobby Vinton?! "Blue Velvet…blue
velvet was her dress…. "I don't mind honoring Johnny
Cash but if I have to hear "the train a comin" one more
time…. Shit. I've saluted every star who's ever been….
Because, since I couldn't finish the tour with you, no
one will book me on my own. The promoters are afraid
only a few thousand fans would come…. So that's
what you've done for me, Carolee—You made me a
casualty of the business. And you won't be satisfied
until I'm truly dead and buried. I was going to do my
new song, *Past Caring*, so the world could see and hear
what Columbia dumped but you won't let me even lick
my wounds.

CAROLEE: (*To herself, audience*) She said to call him
"twelve kinds of asshole". (*To* CHASE) You were in
trouble when I met you…. Don't blame me.

CHASE: A man try to stand, it isn't for a woman to step
on his face. I held you in my arms. That's the wound
that will never heal. And I wanted you to hear it—so
you'd have to face what you done "Past Caring".
That's the place you left me. (*With more emotion than
we've heard before*) "Past Caring!"

CAROLEE: (*Thrown, she doesn't know what she's saying*)
That could be a hit.

CHASE: Not if no one hears it! It's Number nine in
Billboard, moving up with a bullet! It's been awhile
since I been on any list, but the other hit list.

CAROLEE: Can you even believe what you're saying?
Do you really see it that way?

CHASE: A blind man could see what happen here.

CAROLEE: Oh, Lord help me. (*Suspicious, to* CHASE)
Have you been born again, again?

CHASE: When I fell so far, there was no farther to fall, that's when Lord helped me to my feet. Now the only sweet thing left to me is my feeling for Him and all Mankind… *(Sigh)* Poor bastards. It wouldn't hurt you to pray—you might still be saved. He loved the whore, Mary Magdalene.

CAROLEE: The whore! What're you calling me?

CHASE: I'm past insulting any man or any female. I'm past caring.

CAROLEE: Oh, please. Just once in your life, you take a look, man: you take a look at me and you see what you done. I've been travelling on empty since Albuquerque. You had me every which way, and left me for dead. And it's only my body been carried from state to state ever since and I sing any song at all, it's my own dirge. Cause you killed me, man, you killed me!

(CHASE, a touch unnerved, takes another hit, holds the smoke.)

CAROLEE: You see darkly through your own smoke, man, if that's what you remember. You killed me, man, you killed me, and you never even noticed when I died!

CHASE: When was that?

CAROLEE: On May the twelfth, at three A M, in a motel room in Albuquerque. A Howard Johnson. Room 101. *(Softer)* I still have the key. *(Low)* You don't know I almost died in that room?

CHASE: I know you left me for dead. People are still shoveling dirt on me, I look so dead… So don't go twisting it around in your head. I been fooled too many times.

CAROLEE: Bullshit, you been fooled. It was you done all the Foolin' and you claim to be "The King of Feelin".

Well, you're the King of Foolin'. You ought to tell a
woman what comes with you. Tell her how you get.

CHASE: *(More somber, trying to recall)* You were
crashing?

CAROLEE: By myself. *(Reporting to him as if he were
innocent)* It was so cold. I felt like I was lying naked in
a crater on the moon. Was it hours or days or nights? I
don't even know…. *(Small voice)* I really believed you'd
come back. I didn't think you'd do me like that. Even
when you were bad, it was better than when you were
gone. You never been in a room after you've left it.

CHASE: *(A bit tickled, flattered)* Pretty empty, huh?

CAROLEE: You never waited for you to come back. See
my side, Chase. Hear yourself: "Stay here in the bed.
I'll be back. You keep custody of this." *(She flies to the
vanity drawer, whips out a bottle of Hawaiian Eucalyptus
Oil.)*

CHASE: *(In recognition)* Oh Lord. He who cleaveth unto
a woman will not soon be set free. *(He takes the oil
bottle, sniffs it.)* It ain't gone rancid. *(Hopeful)* It's still
good. *(With the possibility of accepting some blame)* Was I
drunk?

CAROLEE: You still are.

CHASE: *(More righteous)* If I did that, that would a been
a terrible, terrible thing, but *(Ever optimistic on his own
behalf)* it ain't like me. I don't think I got that bad.
(Anxious to resume an attack, a defense for himself) You
didn't have to run off with Norbie!

CAROLEE: Norbie! Run off with Norbie? Norbie
picked up the pieces. I was lying there like a broken
doll, when he come by in the morning with an Egg
McMuffin and some fries. And how do you think I
felt: Norbie seeing me in the condition I was? I didn't
even have the strength to put on a disguise. He saw

me naked, and that was thanks to you…. *(New, serious tone)* You know, you don't have to take everything when you go, you could leave a woman with her pride. *(Mustering some strength)* A person has to go on with her life, especially if it ain't just for herself but for her fans, and her family. I never run off with Norbie: He picked up the pieces and has stood with the glue, ever since. I never slept with him, sometimes I let him touch my hair.

CHASE: *(Thrown a bit)* Well, what about what happened to me? I come to an empty motel room, and find a stain upon the bed! *(Recalling)* A big grease spot…

CAROLEE: *(Counterattack)* And when was that? How many hours or how many days later?

CHASE: *(Faltering)* That's a bit unclear.

CAROLEE: Well… You could have called. Or written…

CHASE: I told you: I don' t call or write.

CAROLEE: Oh, and you tell a woman that when she's already half-dead…when you've poured two quarts of tequila into her, and turned her every way but loose…. Why don't you say that for starters…. Mister Honesty… Say, "Hey, Carolee, come to my bed, but if I ain't inside you, Baby, I'm gone!" Tell me, what does your God say to that? Is that one way you help mankind?

CHASE: *(With real menace)* Don't you mock my God.

CAROLEE: You mock your God. Everything you ever sang or said is a lie!

(After this last attack, CAROLEE trembles: she didn't think she had it in her. Now, she breathes hard, waiting for his retort. But instead of fighting back, to her surprise, CHASE crumbles: he kind of folds up, and jackknifes, as though mortally wounded, upon her bed. He hides his head, and appears to be sobbing into her pillow.)

CAROLEE: *(Stunned into solace; soft)* I'm sorry. Now how'd you turn this around? You're still my Baby…. You know that. Some things never change. I'm sorry: I spoke too hard…. I was hurt, I felt bad…. I didn't mean what I was saying. *(Thinking)* It may be you ain't responsible for the harm you done.

CHASE: *(Muffled, but he's easing his head into her lap)* That's what they're saying, saying my songs are lies. And they're all true, it's all true: Those are my real feelings: If I can't speak them at least I thought I could sing…them…. They hit me so hard, Carolee, and for my best work…. They hate what I sing and how I sing it. When I pass through New York last summer, they said in the newspaper, I sound like a "bullmoose in heat."

CAROLEE: *(Laughing: the tension is easing)* Oh, Honey, that's nothing. They say that kind of thing all the time. They told me I sound like a chickadee with a bad cold. *(Pause)* It didn't stop me. Hell, you can't listen to the critics. You know that.

CHASE: *(Little boy voice)* They can kill your fight.

CAROLEE: *(Warming to his defense)* Oh, they don't know nothing. They're jealous, that's all. *(To audience)* They knew where that voice a his was comin' from, they'd be twice as mad.

CHASE: *(Warming, also)* You still listen to me?

CAROLEE: Well, it's hard to…. I start, and the minute I hear your three little chords, you're here in my room. It's like you live in the air, like you're standing here. *(With amused irritation)* You know I had to finish the tour by myself? You left me with seven cities to go. How'd you think I felt, singing both sides of a duet? *(She smiles to disarm him.)* I felt like Doctor Jekyll and Mrs Hyde. The next night, in Tucson, we come on with a cardboard cutout a you. I had to sing to it. *(To*

audience with a bit of the old spite) It showed more feelin.
(Flat, to CHASE*)* I told the audience you had spinal
meningitis.

CHASE: I was drunk.

CAROLEE: *(Cradling him, stroking his hair)* Your hair
feels so good, it smells so clean. *(Resuming business talk)*
Well, I didn't mind doing your medley. I got more
inside your music that way. *(She sings, a peppy tune)*
"Say good bye to everybody. Say hello to every face."

*(*CHASE *responds, snuggling against* CAROLEE*.)*

CHASE: Go on.

CAROLEE: *(Very soft)* It made me feel you was still with
me, still in me, some way.

CHASE: *(Sincere, aroused)* That's nice. *(Sigh, confiding)*
Maybe it was just too easy to take. You on stage with
me, it was a piece of cake. I don't know why I go. *(He
muses.)* Maybe I'm punishing myself for some sin I
can't remember.

CAROLEE: *(Anxious to forgive him)* That's probably it.

*(*CAROLEE *and* CHASE *are both becoming amorous, cuddling
in the bed.)*

CHASE: *(With real charm, smiling up at her)* Well, we sure
could harmonize. *(He means sex.)*

CAROLEE: *(Blushing, aroused; she sings to tease him.)* "Yer
no better than you should be…

CHASE: *(Completing the lyric while he lies on top of her
body)* …But yer good enough for me."

CAROLEE: You are.

CHASE: *(Returning to a bit of a sulk)* I loved every song
you ever sang but the last one…after you left me….

CAROLEE: *(Trying to set the record straight, but speaking softly so as not to kill the romantic mood)* I never left you—you left me! Which song?

CHASE: Jest guess.

CAROLEE: *(Not quite innocent)* I don't have a clue.

CHASE: *(A bit mean, again)* You know which one....

CAROLEE: *(Embarrassed)* Oh, "So long, Fred". *(Struggling to regain his good graces)* I thought of that as kind of a... private joke.... Between you n' me... *(Sadly)* I thought it'd make you laugh, maybe even bring you running. *(Wistful)* "So long, Fred."

CHASE: *(With a touch of the old vehemence)* Everybody knows I call my pecker "Fred"!

CAROLEE: Everybody?

CHASE: Well, enough to make it embarrassing. *(Sad)* A lot of people in the business knew just what you meant. *(With the possibility of reconciliation)* I thought you did it to make me look bad.

CAROLEE: *(Earnest)* Honey, that was as close to a love song as I've ever sung. I was complimenting you! *(She pauses: an afterthought)* ...And Fred.

CAROLEE: *(Softer tone)* I'm sorry if you took it the wrong way. It' s okay. *(Angrier)* But you didn't have to sue me!

CHASE: I didn't sue you, you sued me!

CHASE: *(Flat)* That was lawyers.

CAROLEE: They said you owned more of "You're no better than you ought to be" than me and you know: that ain't so! We were fifty fifty, a straight split!

CHASE: They said you wanted it all.

CAROLEE: I didn't know they said that! *(Trying to resume the romantic mood; softer voice)* What do I know?

Here I am, lying in my bus, *(Flirting)* missing you, dying for the sound of your old voice. I don't know what my lawyers is doing, except stealing my money. I don't even know who they are. You know me and money. I could care less. They couldn't pay me enough do what I do.

CHASE: *(Resuming the embrace)* Me, too.

CAROLEE: *(Really trying to get past the fight)* It's good we talked. It's all been misunderstanding. Third parties coming between our two bodies.

CHASE: Not now.

CAROLEE: No more.

CHASE: *(With touch of old self-righteousness)* So you're sorry. You're apologizing to me.

CAROLEE: *(Unable to apologize)* We have to forgive each other…. We can't be "past caring".

CHASE: I never am with you…. *(Low, sexual, moving in on her. His breathing changes, he lowers his head, has that "meek" look she's described. He tilts his face toward her, the question asked but not spoken.)*

CAROLEE: *(To herself)* Stop me. I can't help myself. The whiskey voice…his hips… *(She catches her breath.)* Your hair… You smell…so…clean….

(CHASE is about to grab CAROLEE, but he wants to seal the deal.)

CHASE: I was just going to say the same thing…. You feel so good…to me…. Nothing ever changes with us; we always feel the same…. *(He is semi-sincere, breathing hard; hot and wanting her in every way.)* I know you won't let me down tonight…it'll be like it was… before…. I want to be with you…. I can't go on stage without you…it'll be like it always was. *(With humor)* You know we got the best duet….

(CHASE *is starting to move against* CAROLEE, *in a swaying full-body caress. She is near-fainting from desire, and losing control of the situation.*)

CHASE: We got to be together again; it sets us right. We'll be real quiet and quick…. (*Sexily but with great humor*) And then everybody can honor us after….

CAROLEE: Oh, my Baby, I'll honor you right now, right here…like you never been honored before….

CHASE: Yer sweet…. Let's just lock the door a minute.

CAROLEE: (*Breathless*) And turn out the light.

(CAROLEE *and* CHASE *kiss, break apart, shivering and laughing. He locks the door, turns down the light. He pulls her dress over her head. Her back is now to the audience. He pulls off his tee shirt. Half naked, he turns toward her. He is very aroused in a stoned, erotic trance.*)

CAROLEE: (*Spontaneous*) I could look at you for a hundred years. (*She turns shy, covers her breasts, looks down at herself. Whispering, for reassurance*) Am I still all right for you?

(CHASE *pauses, displeased;* CAROLEE*'s lost points with her loss of confidence or need for reassurance.*)

CHASE: (*Cool, spontaneously tactless*) I hate that. Woman asked me that in Pasadena last week. Thought I only like teenagers now…and I don't…. (*Stoned mumble*) There was something about her really turned me on….

(CAROLEE *stiffens. A tense second passes. She's offended but too desirous to stop now. Instead of reprimanding* CHASE, *she moves to close the gap. She opens her arms to him, palms exposed.*)

CAROLEE: (*Speaking reflexively, without thought, conciliatory*) You look so wonderful, it got me scairt. That's all. Just for a second. You got me scared.

(CAROLEE *embraces* CHASE, *hides her face in his neck. They pass through the awkward moment, and begin to make love. For all his previously casual manner, he brings a solemn tender lust to the next moments. He takes the time and uses the silence, looking at her, holding her. Lights further dim, as he lowers himself onto her, her head tilting backward off the bed toward the audience.)*

CHASE: *(Rapt, whisper sincere)* There's nothing like this—nothing else gives us this. *(Lowest whisper)* Don't you wish we could stay this way forever....

(From offstage, EARL WAYNE *bellows.)*

EARL WAYNE: Caroleee! It's time!

*(*CHASE *rises, in the stirrups as it were. Lights faintly illuminate him astride* CAROLEE, *resting his weight on his knees. Interrupted at his pleasure, he doesn't dismount, but twists his neck, yelling like a warrior to the enemy behind the door.)*

CHASE: Smart move asshole! I'm in here!

(There is the off stage thunder of EARL WAYNE *fleeing the bus, moving like a heavy animal in flight.* CHASE *takes a second to glare at the door. Still without abandoning his position atop the stunned* CAROLEE, *he has ceased abruptly to make love, but continues a discourse on his problems. She regards the audience, her face upside-down, in ultimate disbelief.)*

CHASE: Shit. I don't get two minutes. This is the goddamned reward. I ain't slept in four days, I think I ate a cheeseburger for breakfast, and...

*(*CHASE *coughs, the motion actually causing secondary ripples within* CAROLEE *who is still quite connected to him. She slightly twitches at each new statement.)*

CHASE: ...now I'm coughing; I think I'm catching a cold. *(He clears his throat, opens his mouth.)*

(CAROLEE *opens her mouth: speechless, a dying guppy, sinking fast.*)

CHASE: I don't know why I'm going out there, they hate my new songs. All they holler for is my old ones, as if I knew what I was doing then. I was twenty. You try and show people how you grow, and they know more than you do…. Don't change your music, it's a built-in bust. You know the latest?

(CAROLEE *cannot react to anything but the fact that* CHASE *is delivering this rap while still on top of her. Her eyes widen.*)

CHASE: The latest is they say I lost my spirit. Where'd I lose it? On Route 208? On the interstate? It ain't a hub cap. I never showed so much a my soul, this is what I get back. (*Not singing, he recites a lyric.*) "Only the one thrills you will kill you…. Only your lover will leave you in pain…. Is there anything colder than the sheets where her warm body has lain?" Then I go into a little lilting thing, some old Scottish ballad my Grandma would sing. You know, I went through Scotland and Wales last summer, and in every little village we would stop, they were singing the old songs…could have been from home….

(*Inquisitive to* CAROLEE, *misreading her stunned response:*)

CHASE: You didn't know they was so close to us? (*Still on his own track; charming, conversational*) Or I guess, it's us, is close to them. (*Righteous*) They come first. (*He swivels, still atop* CAROLEE; *new, pragmatic tone*) You got any cough syrup?

(CAROLEE *makes a minimal motion: a tilt of her head toward the bottle of syrup* HONEY *left behind on the shelf beside the pillow.* CHASE *leans over to look at the syrup, still not severing his connection to her.*)

CHASE: I can't drink this shit…. Maybe some water….

(At last, CHASE lifts himself free of CAROLEE's body. He neatly wraps the sheet around his waist. She marks this motion, by eye-ing the audience: Well, he's finally gotten up. He crawls over her body to reach the tiny sink. He takes a drink from the faucet.)

CHASE: *(Hoarse)* It ain't helping. It's making it worse.

(Now anxious for his voice, CHASE delicately elbows CAROLEE aside, to inspect himself in her vanity mirror. He is surrounded by the blonde wig heads: an impassive gallery. She raises her head weakly to watch him, in continued disbelief. He opens his mouth, inspects his tonsils in the mirror.)

CHASE: I got white spots on my tonsils. An asshole doctor took them out five years ago…in Toledo…. They grew back. *(Pause, as he eyes himself in mirror)* Well, I look like hell. You got some Murine?

(CAROLEE cannot respond. She sags, lying back, her face hanging upside down in direct eye contact with the audience, as CHASE rushes through his grooming above her. He finds the Murine, squirts his eyes, blinks, quick washes with a washcloth; he is restored to professional good looks and re-energized by the coital control he has exercised [if not released].)

CHASE: Better put yer dress back on…. *(He zips up his jeans, with a rueful smile, referring to their coitus interruptus.)* Was going to be a nice one….

(CHASE eyes CAROLEE more critically, as she doesn't respond.)

CHASE: There's a whole bunch of people out there. I Just don't want you to be embarrassed.

CAROLEE: *(To audience, herself)* Embarrassed? *(To CHASE)* I'm past that. That's just the public, that's just the business….

CHASE: You said you were with me….

CAROLEE: I am with you….

CHASE: Then put yer dress back on…

CAROLEE: I got a better idea —tell Earl Wayne, we both took sick. Real sudden. And we have to…stay in bed. And recover. *(She manages a laugh.)* Hell, it's the truth.

CHASE: C'mon, we were doin' fine…. Let's just get up there, and do our duet…and be honored…and git it over with….

CAROLEE: *(Negotiating)* And after the show? *(She means: Will they be together?)*

CHASE: I go to Alberta, Canada. C'mon now. Put yer dress on. We got to go now I can't let 'em say I'm a "no-show"…It'd be a black mark against me in the business. And I can't get no more black marks in this business.

CAROLEE: *(Serious whisper, gesturing to her nakedness)* Is *this* the business?

(The sounds of the auditorium increase, as HONEY *and others can be heard singing out their numbers. A rhythmic clapping starts; we can feel the demand as a physical one— the demand to see the two top stars:* CHASE *and* CAROLEE.*)*

CHASE: *(Coughing)* Where's yer throat spray? See what you done; now I can't even talk, how am I supposed to sing? Gggghhhhhhhh. I sound terrible. Shit, I don't want to go out there….

CAROLEE: Then don't, Baby. What's out there? It's in here. Who needs more? *(Shy confession)* You don't need what they have out there…. Ain't this what all the singing's for? Singing my way, twenty years, just to get over to you… *(She laughs at herself.)* It's getting so I can't tell the difference anymore. I don't know if it's my heart or my career. *(To audience)* Well, I can sing or I can cry, can't I?

CHASE: I ain't going to beg you, Carolee. How the hell am I going to look, singing both sides of a duet?

CAROLEE: Like I did in Albuquerque.

CHASE: Audience is like an animal out there. Let's not make 'em any madder… *(Groping for his stuff)* I had my case.

CAROLEE: Make sure you take it all this time. Don't leave anything behind. Except me.

CHASE: Shit. *(He paces, trying to think of some way to budge her.)* What if I get the shakes up there? Will that make you happy? Remember Omaha. I was shaking like a dog trying to shit a peach pit. The audience hated me from the start, so I started shaking harder…. Nothing stinks up there like the fear…. They won't forgive you for fear…. You helped me out in Omaha. You reached out your hand to me. And we sang my song together….

CAROLEE: That's how I got stuck with you. An' you put things so pretty. Well, I changed my mind. I ain't going on. You took everything else. Leave me my pride. This is the one thing I have left…. I only sing a song that's true. That's what I get to offer. I don't fake it on stage, like some others I can name. I could only sing with you, if it was true! But the way you been behaving, it's the same damn lies, it always is. I guess this is a lesson I had to learn over again…but I just learned it real good…so good bye. You're on your own….

(CHASE starts kicking walls and spinning around in a fury.)

CHASE: That's five! Leadin' me on tonight. No, that's six, there was gettin' Honey to trick me onto your bus—and make it seven, for catching me with my pants down and my feelings showin'!

CAROLEE: Stop it. Don't go flipping out now. You can go on without me.

CHASE: *(Ugly paranoid imitation singing)* You're no better than you ought to be, *(He mimics her voice.)* …but you're good enough for me…" *(Deadly)* You just can't get enough a hurting me. Just out to screw me one more time.

EARL WAYNE: *(Offstage)* Oh, Mister McCain…. Uh, your band's on stage now; doin' yer medley. Uh, any time now, we can't hold it any longer…. Carolee—they are callin' for you…!

(Sounds rise; the irritated whistles and calls from the audience.)

CHASE: Shut up, Ass Hole, I'll be there when I'm there! *(To* CAROLEE*)* Now, the band, the whole fuckin' world's laughin' at me…. Well, I guess I'm lucky this is all you do to me. When you could just have me snuffed.

("Snuffed" hangs in the air—like dirty smoke, revealing the criminal capacity in CHASE *himself, the depths of his paranoia.)*

CAROLEE: *(Weakened by the word)* "Snuffed"? Killed?

CHASE: Then you have it all, and it's more than thirty pieces a silver. Judas Escariot took thirty pieces a silver, but you'll get a lot more. I'm gone, got rid of…. Don't you know I can feel it? Yer thoughts are knives in my back, I can't turn around on stage without feeling, the hate stab me in the kidneys….

CAROLEE: *(Shocked into comforting him out of his delusion)* No, don't think those thoughts. There's no hate. Don't you know, Man, don't you know? You got all the love…?

(Sounds of fans screaming for CHASE, CAROLEE*)*

CAROLEE: Listen, they love you! They want to see you! You'll be fine without me! Just tell them…tell 'em. I had some kind of an attack. Tell 'em I got heart trouble.

CHASE: *(Coming around a bit)* All right.

CAROLEE: It's true…. I been pushing' myself too hard this trip.

CHASE: *(With that sexual feeling)* Yeah, and we were cruising close to crazy and I'm in Canada tonight, Detroit tomorrow… *(He moves away.)* And I can hardly walk. I got blue balls. Fred's never been so sore. I feel like I been through a meat grinder. That's *eight* things I'll never do again when I'm on tour…. Get next to someone who's mad at me, just before I have to go on…

CAROLEE: *(To audience)* Let me die…. Let me die, now. *(To* CHASE*)* You are…twelve kinds of asshole! I'd be scairt to stay with you!

CHASE: *(Responding favorably of course as* HONEY *predicted)* Well thank you, Darlin'. You're very good at making me feel desirable, but women's afraid of staying' together, the way flies are afraid of horseshit.

CAROLEE: It ain't romantic, but it's true. *(She's startled into laughing.)*

(From outside, CHASE*'s theme plays.)*

*(*CHASE *flips* CAROLEE *the oil bottle.)*

CHASE: These long road tours. Here, keep the oil. Maybe our paths will cross again. So much shit in here… *(He seems stunned, disoriented, stumbling around, picking up his guitar, and bumping his head as he opens the wrong door—an ironing board hits him.)* Yer ironing board almost knocked me out.

CAROLEE: You need some help finding the door?

CHASE: *(With a whisper, a grin, recovering, he exits)* The one thing, I can always find.

(The instant the door shuts, CAROLEE *falls back on the bed, face-up as if she has, in a serio/comic way, dropped*

dead from the experience. She does not cry, but stiffens in place. Lavender light suffuses the room, stripes through her window. She lies flat, the dress on top of her body, like a corpse at a wake. The neon reflection evokes her nightmare— that she will die of heartbreak, tonight and be laid out in a "wine-colored coffin" in a "wine-color room." Sounds of show in progress)

EARL WAYNE: Carolee! Carolee! I ain't callin' you again....

(The door opens and NORBIE *flies in, at his most distraught.)*

NORBIE: Carolee! Carolee. Come on. You can't kid around no more. *(He bends over, shocked by her apparition-like quality.)* Are you dead or sleeping?

(Seeing that CAROLEE *breathes:)*

NORBIE: Carolee, this is serious, now. That sunofabith just come out and told everybody you can't come on; you got a kidney stone, and yer in here, passing it....

*(*CAROLEE *bolts up, wide-eyed.)*

NORBIE: And Honey Bascomb is up there, all set to accept the award in yer behalf....

(This news reactivates CAROLEE *completely.)*

EARL WAYNE: *(Off. Blaring on the intercom)* This ain't professional!

CAROLEE: What's professional? A whore's professional! All "professional" means is you take money for it!

*(*CAROLEE *fies into action: flinging on hairpieces, the dress.* NORBIE *aids her, in a total frenzy.)*

CAROLEE: Do me up in back! Norbie? You do something for me? Go back out there. You tell 'em, you tell 'em all: Caroleee Crockett is doing her concert...for free....

NORBIE: You got to pay back Barney…. A hundred thousand!

CAROLEE: That'd be cheap. Go on… *Run!* Tell 'em, tell 'em to come out here. By my bus. Tell 'em, Carolee don't do her fans that way. Tell 'em I ain't passing no kidney stone. I'm fine, and I'm giving them my show…. *(Proud)* And not for no T V.

NORBIE: And I don't have to suck hind tit no more?

CAROLEE: This ain't the time, Norbie. We'll talk about it later. I'll raise you up a couple a hundred a month.

NORBIE: You know that ain't what I want…. I want…

(CAROLEE moves past NORBIE, toward the audience.)

CAROLEE: Oh, Norbie…don't pull nothing now…I need you to do this real bad, like I never wanted anything more before in my life!

NORBIE: I hear you, I hear you.

(NORBIE runs out, en route to the stage.)

(CAROLEE, in highest gear, puts finishing touches to her violet dress, fusses with her long hair. She dons a straw hat, with ribbons, faces the audience.)

EARL WAYNE: *(Off)* Wal, this is jest great, Carolee, you have to do us this way. You ain't the only one on this gig.

CAROLEE: You'll git your money, Earl Wayne; that's how you're thinking. This one's for me. You all tell 'em…. "Just stand right out here by my bus", they'll see a show. That's where I'll be…. They want to hear my medley; that's where I'll be. *(She turns direct to the audience, takes a step toward them. With the highest spirit, and a soaring voice, she throws up her arms, wide.)* You all jest holler. Holler whut you want to hear. *(The tears, long held in check, shine in her eyes. Her smile, her song, is*

ecstatic. This is her victory. Full out, radiant:) You all jest
holler! Holler whut you want to hear!

(Blackout)

END OF PLAY

www.ingramcontent.com/pod-product-compliance
Lightning Source LLC
Chambersburg PA
CBHW070032110426
42741CB00035B/2743